$2.95

Angel of Mercy

The Story of Dorothea Lynde Dix

Angel of Mercy

The Story of Dorothea Lynde Dix

by Rachel Baker

Julian Messner, Inc. New York

Published by Julian Messner, Inc.
8 West 40th Street, New York 18

Published simultaneously in Canada
by The Copp Clark Company, Ltd.

© Copyright 1955 by Rachel Baker

Printed in the United States of America

Library of Congress Catalog Card No. 55-9849

Fourth Printing, 1959

Property of
Trinidad High
School Library

14,542

To those

"Angels of Mercy"

everywhere

BOOKS BY RACHEL BAKER

ANGEL OF MERCY: *The Story of Dorothea Lynde Dix*

SIGMUND FREUD

CHAIM WEIZMANN: *Builder of a Nation*

DR. MORTON: *Pioneer in the Use of Ether*

THE FIRST WOMAN DOCTOR: *The Story of Elizabeth Blackwell, M.D.*

Contents

To Those for Whom I Write

This is not a book about a woman who built in wood or stone. This is not a book about a woman who built thirty great mental hospitals in America and several more in Europe.

This is a story about a woman who built in more than wood and stone. This is a story about a woman who built in idea.

She left the idea that no one is so mentally twisted, so tormented he should be failed by our compassion. She left the idea that it is not enough to take sick people out of dungeons and give them clean beds.

She left the idea that they must never become "cases" receiving only efficient treatment; they need love.

And when the hospitals she built became institutions, she descended with fury—calling for bright paper on the walls, warm carpets, cheerful pictures; but most of all for loving attitudes, human warmth and compassion, which the sick need more than all other kinds of care.

She left the idea that we must have no more "snake pits" either physical or mental; that we must have no more unloving attitudes toward the emotionally disturbed.

Her work, then, shall go on until her great idea is

realized—the idea of love and kindness and warmth and mercy.

For help in writing this book I am indebted to many persons: to my husband and my editor for their criticism; to my daughter, Joanna Baker, for her research and for her discovery of a very valuable and hitherto unknown letter written by Dorothea Lynde Dix to Horace Mann.

I want to thank Richard Gallant, an officer of the Middlesex County House of Correction and Jail in East Cambridge, who took me by matchlight through those dark underground cells which first inspired Dorothea Lynde Dix.

I want to thank Mrs. Grinnell Willis, an inspired librarian, and the staff members of the Ferguson Library in Stamford. I am especially grateful to the staff of the New Jersey State Hospital in Trenton for pictures, mementos of Miss Dix, and for showing me the apartment in the tower where she spent the last years of her life. May this apartment be preserved as a national memorial.

Let me thank a little girl in Iowa, one of my readers, who asked me to write another book "about a great woman." I wrote this book to please her.

Stamford, Connecticut
May, 1955

RACHEL BAKER

Angel of Mercy

The Story of Dorothea Lynde Dix

1

Little Girl Lost

The coach tossed in darkness. The little girl slept, woke, slept, then woke again. The two farm women beside her kept on talking in gusty whispers.

"So you're taking the child to Boston?"

"Aye, her father has had one of his spells."

"Spells do you call them? I would call it—"

"Nay, nay, the poor man has a torment in his head!"

"Then let his father cure him with cupping or with leeches." The woman laughed. The child in the darkness clenched her hands. The coach rushed on.

The next day in Boston one of the women took the

little girl by the hand. They climbed the steps of a big red brick house with a tall cupola.

A maid in stiff skirts, a cap like a tumbler on her head, opened the door. She sighed reprovingly, "Again?"

She took the little girl upstairs. She scrubbed her. She curled her hair into tight black corkscrews. She buttoned her into a quilted frock and pantalets so glossy with starch that the ruffles stood out like porcelain.

She told the child, "Go downstairs and greet your grandmother."

By the drawing-room window sat a woman in a brocaded gown, her dark hair dressed high. A big, square cameo hung from a black ribbon at her throat. She was sewing on a bit of fine linen, her needle moving like a lance.

"My bitter namesake!" she sighed.

The little girl sat down on a polished stool by her grandmother. Her grandmother kept sewing. The little girl sewed too. She sewed with crooked stitches on a sampler which read "God Bless Our Home."

Many times her grandmother made the child take the stitches out, saying as she often did when the little girl came to visit, "Here you will have to learn to do things properly."

Here the velvet curtains hung at the windows in

exact folds. The silver tea service on a corner table gleamed so the child could see herself in the teapot with her eyelids and cheeks elongated, her face drawn out in a strange way.

When her fingers and her back ached from sewing, the little girl went to the window. She watched the sick people who came to the side of the house to see her grandfather.

Her grandmother said, "Come away from the window."

Later the little girl's grandfather came into the house. He wore white gaiters and a broad-brimmed hat. He smelled of unguents as he kissed the child.

He said, "I am going to the apothecary shop on Milk Street."

The little girl pulled on his hand.

"Very well," he said, "come along then."

They drove down Washington Street, her grandfather sitting in the open carriage, his hands on his goldheaded cane, his face looking gray and worried as it always did when the little girl came to stay with him.

They stopped at the foot of Milk Street and he told the coachman to wait. They walked along the twisting street, where the May morning shadows still lay on the cobblestones.

They passed the dim shops of the mercer, the draper, and the tallowmaker. Then the little girl saw, far down the street, a sign that she knew—a stone mortar and pestle hanging on an iron rod, the sign of the apothecary.

She gave a slight shiver. "Grandfather," she said, "will I see the leeches and may I touch them?"

He looked at her surprised. "Touch the leeches? Of course not. They would suck your blood. And I doubt that you need any bloodletting."

She stopped him in the door of the shop. He glanced at her with a frown, as if knowing that she worried. He had his hand on the latch, but he did not go into the shop. She lifted dark lashes to regard him.

"Grandfather, what is bloodletting for?"

"Why, to draw out bad humors, of course."

"All kinds of humors and torments?" she asked tensely.

"Aye," he frowned.

She seemed to hesitate. Then desperately in a very low voice she said, "Could the leeches draw out a torment from here?" And she pointed to her forehead.

He gazed at her aghast, then turned his face away twisted with pain. "Nay, child, nay," he said wearily, "I know of no power of leeches strong enough to pull out the torments from your father's poor head!"

"Nor medicines, nor unguents?" she urged.

He hurried into the shop without answering. She followed him into the acrid dimness. The apothecary, a long, thin man with a lean, folded face, rose unctuously to greet them.

"Ah, Dr. Dix! And is this your little granddaughter who has come all the way from Maine to visit you?"

"Aye, my granddaughter, Dorothea Lynde Dix," said Dr. Dix curtly.

The child went to stare at a bowl of leeches which stood near the window.

"Then this must be the daughter of your son Joseph and that Bigelow woman he married," the apothecary said, in a whisper.

Dr. Dix did not answer.

The apothecary began to grind up bitter aloes. "Ah, what a sad marriage!" he said, holding the mortar to his breast. "A young man like that, a student at Harvard, and a farm woman twice as old as he—old enough to be his mother."

A bitter smell filled the shop.

"Tell me, sir," the apothecary suggested, "is it true that your son gives up his intemperate ways now and then, to preach in the streets and give out tracts on salvation?"

The apothecary lifted his face in a strange sidelong way to Dr. Dix, who did not speak but only held onto the golden knob of his cane more tightly.

"People tell me, sir, that when your son is himself he can be very eloquent."

The old man gave a bitter sigh. "Whatever he does is done with equal intemperance."

The child, who had been looking with stinging eyelids at the leeches, whirled around. "You shouldn't talk about my father that way," she sobbed. "He has a torment in his head, and if you were a good doctor you would cure him instead of blaming him."

Her grandfather made no answer. In silence the apothecary measured out the powders he had ground. The little girl and her grandfather drove home in silence.

That night as the child lay in her room she heard her grandfather and grandmother talking in agitated tones as they came upstairs.

"The child is unruly and she should be curbed," said Madame Dix in a high, precise voice.

"Did you curb your son?" asked Dr. Dix wearily.

"Don't call him son," Madame Dix cried out. "I have no son!" And she passed with a rustle of silk down the hall.

Many years later the child was to fully learn her history, and the many strange events that had led to the hatred which, like a bad dream, had filled all her childhood.

It began with the big red brick house on Orange Court where Madame Dix lived with her husband, Dr. Elijah Dix, and their many spoiled sons.

Several of these sons left home, to die violent deaths —one in Canada, one in Kentucky, one in the West Indies. The fourth son, Joseph, a frail, tormented youth haunted by religious visions, wanted to be a minister, instead of a physician as his father had hoped.

The young man entered Harvard at seventeen. He made his parents angry by leaving the Calvinistic religion they observed. He talked about a great preacher, Charles Wesley, of whom he had heard. He told his parents he wanted to become a wandering preacher too, to bring God to the people in the streets.

They became still more angry with him. They told him people brought up properly did not do such things. He was filled with despair. The gates of heaven seemed to close for him. He found his way to taverns and he took to drinking.

No one knows where the next adventure of his life happened, whether in a tavern or at a revival meeting. He met a farm woman from Sudbury, a small village just outside of Cambridge.

Maybe she was kind to him. Maybe she was motherly. Maybe she believed in the gates of the heaven about which he talked wildly. Maybe she too sought those gates of heaven. But when she too could not find them, she took refuge in many ailments.

The young man and the elderly nervous woman

were married. The young man was expelled from Harvard, for it was the rule in those days that no student could marry and remain at school.

When Madame Dix heard that her son Joseph, aged eighteen, had married Mary Bigelow, near to forty, she said with great bitterness to her husband, "Send the two of them as far from Boston as you can!"

Dr. Dix owned a tract of wilderness on the Penobscot River in Maine, then not yet a state. There he had laid out the settlements of Dixfield and Dixmount. There he hoped someday to sell land and grow richer.

He sent Joseph and his wife to Hampden, a crossroads village in the wilderness, not far from Bangor and halfway between Dixfield and Dixmount. There his son was supposed to act as a kind of land agent for him.

Joseph, however, more tormented than before, sold no land. Sometimes he wrote tracts on salvation which he distributed to the farmers. Sometimes he stayed too long in distant taverns. His wife surrounded herself with more medicine bottles.

In their cottage, where tracts and dirty dishes littered the table, often the sound of quarreling was heard. In this cottage on April 4, 1802, their first child was born, a little girl. Joseph with sick longing named his child Dorothea Lynde Dix, for his mother.

Thereafter in times of trouble he sent the child to

his parents in Boston; so the little girl passed the first seven years of her life tossed between the slatternly cottage in Hampden and the big correct house on Orange Court which everyone in Boston called "Dix Mansion."

In the summer of 1809 the little girl stayed in Boston with her grandparents for several weeks. During this time two things happened which she was always to remember.

One day her grandfather took her to the docks to see loads of chemicals being shipped off to England from his factory in South Boston, for he was a person of great enterprise.

As the horses panting under their heavy loads came past the end of Milk Street which lies near to the docks, Dr. Dix said, frowning, "Someone should put up a fountain here so all the thirsty horses can drink."

At another time Dr. Dix took his little granddaughter out to the big cavernous stable behind Dix Mansion. Lifting her up, he let her stroke the velvety noses of his new carriage horses, lovely silky brown animals who quivered when she touched them.

When the time came for the little girl to go back to Hampden, her grandfather lifted her into the coach. For a moment he held her in his arms, his shoulders strangely quivering.

"I hope I shall be here when you come back."

The little girl did not see her grandfather again. That summer he passed away while on a journey to Maine to look after his lands, and he was buried in Dixmount.

After that, Dorothea heard dimly of a letter her grandmother had sent to Hampden which said, "I refuse to have anything more to do with the loveless home which my son's folly and weakness has created."

Then Dorothea's parents moved from Hampden. They moved with Dorothea and her two little brothers, Joseph and Charles Wesley, to the village of Bernard, in Vermont.

They settled in a broken-down cottage near the meetinghouse. There Dorothea had to go from house to house with a handbill which read, "Books from Boston, sold at cheap prices. Farm vegetables and produce taken in exchange."

But not all the books which Dorothea's father tried to sell came from Boston. She knew some of them came from a box which he called "my Harvard box," and which no one had ever been allowed to touch except Dorothea.

She learned to read from the books in this box, spelling out the big words. And when her father felt happy he held her on his knee and taught her.

For a little while, in Bernard, Dorothea went to school. But she could read, write, and cipher much faster than all the other children. Besides, she did not like any of the other children. Sometimes they followed her father in the streets and pointed to their foreheads.

Dorothea taught her little brothers, Joseph, aged seven, and Charles Wesley, aged four, spelling out the letters for them or else telling them stories.

When Dorothea was ten years old she heard a great deal about another war with England, and the British who would march from Canada and burn down all their homes.

Many people fled from Bernard, which lay in the mountains close to Canada. Finally Dorothea's parents fled too. They went to Worcester, Massachusetts, a city of which Dorothea had heard, and where once, long ago, her grandmother had been known as the "belle of Worcester."

There Madame Dix had been the beautiful daughter of Joseph Lynde, one of the proudest citizens in the town. There her sisters had married into the most prominent families of the town: the Duncans, the Bangses, and the Wheelers.

Dorothea had heard of "great-aunt Sarah Duncan," who lived in a big white house on a hill, and of "great-uncle Judge Bangs," who told everyone in Worcester what to do.

When Dorothea moved with her parents and brothers to Worcester, they lived in a tumble-down cottage at the edge of town. For some reason Dorothea's father went more than ever to taverns, and her mother lay sick more than ever with retching headaches. She complained over and over that she had no strength for the children.

One day rich relatives appeared at the house—a dark-haired woman with a big green silk calabash on her head which looked like a pumpkin, and a man with a goldheaded cane and a big chin pressed into a huge satin stock.

Dorothea recognized her great-aunt Sarah Duncan, and her great-uncle Judge Bangs. They seemed to know what everyone should do.

They sent Dorothea's father and mother off in a closed carriage, to New Hampshire, to board with a distant relative of Dorothea's mother who said she would look after them, for a fee.

Then they sent Dorothea and her two brothers off to Boston, to Dix Mansion, to be brought up properly by their grandmother.

The three ragged children faced their grandmother in the drawing room. Dorothea at once pushed herself in front of her two brothers—Joseph, a silent boy of eight, Charles Wesley, a frightened, pale child of five.

Madame Dix sighed, "To think that at seventy I must start to bring up another family!"

She sent Joseph off to Latin School. She hired a nurse for Charles Wesley. She looked at Dorothea, a tall, thin, scowling girl of twelve, whose dark, tumbled hair fell over angry blue eyes fringed with long dark lashes.

With decision Madame Dix said, "You must learn to stand properly. You must learn to walk properly. In two years you shall be a belle."

A struggle began. . . .

Madame Dix hired a dancing master for Dorothea. Dorothea said he hopped like a frog. "Moreover, I intend to do something useful."

Madame Dix hired a seamstress for Dorothea. Dorothea left the new gowns hanging in her closet and wore one old dress poked out at the sleeves, until Madame Dix in a rage tore this gown from her back. Then Dorothea put on one of the new fine frocks, first tearing off all the ribbons.

Dorothea read incessantly. She fed the beggar children at the gate. "What do you want to do?" Madame Dix cried. "Bring a pestilence into the house?"

Madame Dix hired fiddlers and gave an assembly, inviting young ladies from the best families to dance the new country dances. Dorothea stood scowling against the wall and would not move.

Madame Dix sent for her sister, Mrs. Sarah Duncan of Worcester. "What's to be done with this girl?"

Mrs. Duncan adjusted her long silk boa, raised her eyebrows, and asked, "How old is the girl now?"

"Fourteen," replied Madame Dix.

"Fourteen!" cried Mrs. Duncan. "Why, then I know what's the matter. It's the *green* years. My daughter had them."

She offered to take Dorothea to Worcester to live with her in the big white house on the hill, always filled with relatives.

So Dorothea was ordered to pack. She did so scowling deeply. Many years later someone was to ask her about her childhood. She seemed surprised.

"Childhood? I never had one!"

2

The Pear Tree Blooms

Mrs. Duncan climbed the stairs to Dorothea's room. "Dorothea," she cried, breathing hard, her bracelets tinkling, "aren't you ready yet?"

Dorothea, barely hearing, dug her elbows into a book she had brought from the Worcester library—a book on the wonders of wind and weather.

"What?"

"Oh, Dorothea! What shall I do with you? Look at your dress! Look at your hair! The guests for tea will be here any moment."

Mrs. Duncan left, her skirts rustling on the stairs. Dorothea put her book down and, with a tug at her hair, which hung in a dark mane down her back, and a jerk at her dress, she went to the top of the stairs.

How she hated these Sunday afternoons when all the rich relatives gathered for tea, when the tea service glittered and the hubbub of talk rose higher and she felt ever more like a stranger!

She sighed and started down the stairs. In the upper gloom she stopped. Below, Judge Bangs had just arrived, in a waistcoat with immense shoulders, his forceful chin sunk in a huge silken stock. Behind him came a tall, handsome man with golden earlocks, his son Edward, an attorney. He gave the maid his pale yellow gloves and then passed on with his father to the dining room.

Dorothea waited like a shadow on the stairs until all the guests had arrived—Mrs. Duncan's married daughter, Mrs. Fiske, and then Mrs. Duncan's younger sister, Mrs. Wheeler, who came with two little girls dressed in white pinafores.

The maid carried away the cloaks, galoshes, and umbrellas, for it had been raining slightly. Dorothea slipped through the hall and into the library, where she sat down on a deep window seat to look out pensively at the dripping lawn.

Two little girls of about six and seven peered into the library. They rushed to the window seat. "Tell us a story," they cried.

"Nancy! Frances!" Dorothea smiled and hugged

them as they climbed onto the window seat, snuggling down beside her, winsome little girls with glossy black curls tumbling in every direction.

Dorothea's face glowed. With children she felt at ease. "What kind of story do you want this time?" But before they could answer, she began to trace the course of a raindrop on the windowpane.

"I will tell you the story of this raindrop," she offered. They pasted their noses to the window. In an enthusiastic voice she began. "Once there was a little raindrop floating way up high in the sky, in a big fleecy white cloud."

She told the little girls how more and more raindrops gathered in this cloud until the cloud grew dark and heavy, so heavy that all the raindrops started to drop to the earth.

Some fell on flowers, and some on rocks, and some on the earth. The flowers drank up the raindrops and in time the raindrops passed into the earth, deep down where springs gathered, far under the ground.

"And then?" the little girls asked.

"These springs flowed into ponds and rivers and lakes and oceans and, as the sun shone, the raindrops danced on top of the water."

"And then?"

"The sun shone brighter and brighter. The raindrops grew lighter and lighter. The raindrops danced up into the air and up into the sky, and up into a fleecy white cloud which was floating by.

"And then?" cried the little girls, their noses still pasted to the windowpane where the pensive raindrops slid.

"And then?" echoed a male voice behind them.

Dorothea jumped up. "You were eavesdropping," she said accusingly.

"Oh no, I was looking for my gloves!" It was her cousin Edward Bangs, really her second cousin, tall and golden, looking for his gloves. He found them on a low table by the door where the maid had put them for safekeeping, immaculate gloves without a fold.

"There, you see."

She scowled, still suspicious.

"That was a very interesting story you told," he assured her. "I recognize the facts to be true."

"Of course," she said. "I don't like made-up stories."

As if questioning a recalcitrant witness, he very gently prodded her for the source of her scientific information. She told him a book on meteorology.

He seemed amazed and said with genuine enthusiasm, "Then you are a born teacher."

"I, a teacher?" Some of her resentment dropped away. "How is that possible?"

"Of course. There are your pupils on the window seat."

The little girls began to clamor immediately for another story. They tugged at her hands. She did not seem to notice them.

Her cousin spoke a while longer and left, holding his gloves in his hand. She gazed at the empty doorway, a deep wrinkle of wonderment on her forehead.

After that, when he came to Sunday tea at the Duncans', as he did frequently with his father, Edward always took time to seek out Dorothea and talk to her.

The others thought this kind of him. "He has a way with people." At twenty-eight he had already climbed high in politics, working hand in hand with General Levi Lincoln, of whom it was said that he would someday be the Governor of Massachusetts.

One day Edward suggested to Dorothea, "Why don't you start a little dame school?"

"Where? How?"

He explained that children in Massachusetts could not go to public school until they had learned to "read Scripture properly."

"Is that why poor children never get to school?" she asked.

Her question glanced off.

He told her that many well-to-do families would welcome a dame school where their children could be taught interestingly.

As a matter of fact, he went on to confide, the Dix

relatives alone would furnish her with enough pupils. As for himself, he might even help. Already he had spoken to his friend General Lincoln, who had promised to send his two little boys, Levi and William.

"To my school?" Her cheeks glowed.

That autumn, in a room which Edward had secured for her, over a bookstore on Main Street, Dorothea, not yet fifteen years old, faced her first pupils.

Among them, on that autumn day in 1816 when she began to teach with a strange confidence, were the two little Wheeler girls, Nancy and Frances; little Joseph Eaton, and Anne Bancroft; Lucy Green; and the two little Lincoln boys, both "imps of devilment."

When Dorothea could not keep the attention of her pupils in any other way, she told them stories about the wonders of everyday life.

She told about the wonders of coal, wood, wind, rain, and stars. She told how rocks were shaped, how flowers grow, and how the light of the Milky Way comes from heaven. The children asked her questions and she answered them. After a time she wrote down the questions and answers in a notebook which she called *Conversations on Common Things.*

When her cousin Edward came to see her, as he did almost every day after school, she told him happily about her teaching.

She told him how she punished a little girl by making her walk around with a placard on her chest which said, "I am a bad child."

He laughed, "Do you think we might do the same with our criminals, shame them into good behavior?"

"Why not?"

"Do you think that we would need no more lashes?"

She shuddered, "I hate cruelty!"

One day when everything had gone particularly well at school, she confided happily to her cousin Edward, "I could go on teaching all the rest of my life!"

He gave a little sigh. "Many girls teach for a year or two before they marry."

She scowled darkly. "I'll never marry!"

He stood in the doorway of the schoolroom flicking his palm with his pale yellow gloves. "I understand how you feel," he said in a rather thoughtful voice. For the first time she noticed a fleck of white in his golden earlocks.

"I used to feel the same way," he went on. "But now that I am almost thirty, living alone does not seem so pleasant."

She began busily to clean off her desk.

For three years she taught happily in Worcester. On a beautiful afternoon in 1820, when she was seventeen years old, her cousin Edward walked home with her one day, as was now his habit.

They passed the green lawns dotted with hot yellow

buttercups and dandelions gleaming like golden pennies. They stopped at her aunt's gate by a wisteria bush heavy with rich purple blossoms which poured a scent almost like wine into the air.

Dorothea opened the high collar of her severe gray gown. Her dark, heavy hair, held in a tight braid twisted like a cart wheel at the back of her head, slipped down and hung more luxuriously between her shoulders.

She took out her handkerchief and fanned herself lightly. The sweet smell of the blossoms made her dizzy. She half closed her eyes.

"What a day!"

Edward dropped his pale yellow immaculate gloves into the dust and for some reason did not pick them up. "Dorothea," he said in a strange voice, as though the blossoms too had made him dizzy, "Dorothea, how long will you continue to teach?"

She looked at him bewildered.

"Dorothea," he cried, and in his agitation he stepped on his pale yellow gloves without noticing them. "I am twice as old as you are. . . ."

She shivered as if at a sound she had heard before. She put her hands to her face and ran into the house. That night she did not sleep. The next day she closed her school in Worcester and fled to Boston.

Edward's letters followed her, and then he came.

They walked in the garden where the pear trees, covered with white blossoms, glowed like tapers. They became engaged.

But even as Dorothea told Edward she would marry him, she heard herself saying, "Not now. First let me teach a while."

He agreed to wait, but reminded her of his age—past thirty.

"Oh, age, age!" she cried. "I feel a hundred years old sometimes!"

She begged her grandmother to let her open a little dame school in the gardener's cottage behind the house. Madame Dix agreed. Dorothea's classes drew so many pupils she could not teach them all in the gardener's cottage, and so after a time she conducted classes in the house.

One day Edward happily confided that his friend General Lincoln might be elected Governor of Massachusetts. "And, if so, I shall be his Secretary of State."

Dorothea suggested, "Then perhaps someday you shall be governor."

"And you a governor's lady," he smiled.

She gave him a gloomy glance. "I don't like to dress up and impress people."

"We do for those we love."

She sighed strangely. . . .

On April 2, 1821, just before Dorothea's nineteenth

birthday, the news came that her father had passed away in New Hampshire.

She met Edward in the garden, her face cold and stern. "Now I know that I will never be able to love anyone."

He pleaded with her. He explained that she was only upset, that she was suffering from nerves, that he would wait a year or two longer, "even though I have not too much time to wait."

She turned her face from him by the blooming pear tree. She heard the gate close. She went into the house. Her grandmother faced her with fury.

"You will never make such a match again in your life."

"Leave me alone!" Dorothea cried.

She threw herself into her work. She taught at her school in Dix Mansion. She taught at Mr. Fowle's Monitorial School for Young Ladies.

She took out the notebook she had started in Worcester. She wrote a book, *Conversations on Common Things,* which a publisher accepted immediately and which was to be reprinted all the years of her life, running through some sixty editions.

She attended lectures on botany, mineralogy, and astronomy. She took private lessons in French from a tutor, Mr. Wentz.

She sought the solace of religion. She left her grandmother's church on Hollis Street and went to hear the minister of the Unitarian Church, Dr. William Ellery Channing, a small man whose face shown like a star. He taught love of mankind. He taught that all must be loved, the sick, the insane, the criminal.

In this church Dorothea saw dedicated human beings—men struggling to make the world over, with their actions and with their thoughts.

Someone pointed out Ralph Waldo Emerson, a preacher with a leaning toward philosophy; and John Greenleaf Whittier, a little, twisted, dark-haired newspaperman who wrote poetry.

She heard of the radiant widower Horace Mann, who struggled so that every child in America should have a free education. She heard of the frail physician Dr. Samuel Gridley Howe, who fought to help the Greeks win their freedom; who carried help to the embattled Poles; and who now, in his father's house, taught little blind children to read with their fingers.

She saw all these people from afar. She did not dare to speak to anyone. But one day in the church parlors on Federal Street the minister's wife, tall, tart Mrs. Channing, whose salty manner hid great warmth of heart, came up to her.

"Miss Dix," she said, "I would like to solicit your interest for a girl who is so shy she sits quite by herself. I wonder if you might not befriend her."

Dorothea gave Mrs. Channing a glance of amazement which the other seemed not to notice. She took Dorothea to a corner of the room where sat a girl with a sweet, shy face, and brown eyes so diffident she hardly dared to look up.

"This is Ann Heath," Mrs. Channing said. "I know that she will be interested in whatever you have to tell her."

To her own surprise Dorothea found herself talking eagerly. She told Ann Heath about her school, about the book she had written, about the other books she hoped to write.

"I am not nearly so clever," said Ann. "All I can do is sew." And she told Dorothea how she made all the clothes for her sisters and brothers and cousins, with whom she lived in a big farmhouse in Brookline.

They became friends. Sometimes Dorothea went to Brookline. "In such a home as yours," she confided to Ann, "I might even be happy." It was a warm home filled with many happy children.

Dorothea sent many notes to her friend Ann, scribbling them during the day on bits of paper which she sewed together with colored thread.

"I have sent you many notes," she wrote Ann sometime later. "We have exchanged many confidences."

She had even told Ann of her engagement to Edward and said that she did not know why she had feared to marry him, because she still missed him greatly. And once she confessed that she could not, even now, bear to look at the pear trees in her grandmother's garden.

"I hate them when they bloom!"

She told Ann how she longed to devote her life to some great and useful work. She told her about the beggar children at the gate of Dix Mansion whose suffering had always moved her greatly.

She told her about a book she had recently read which was the life story of a great woman, Hannah More. This woman had left London and the society of Garrick, Sir Joshua Reynolds, and the noted Dr. Johnson and buried herself in the impoverished Mendip Hills country, where she started schools for beggar children.

"If I could only do something like that!" Dorothea cried one day.

"Why not?" suggested Ann gently.

Dorothea persuaded her grandmother to go with her just once to hear Dr. Channing. And she begged her grandmother to read just one book, the life of Hannah More.

Not trusting herself to speak, Dorothea then wrote her grandmother a letter. "My dear Grandmother," she began. "Had I the saintlike eloquence of our minister, I would employ it in explaining all the good,

good to the poor, the miserable, the idle, and the ignorant, which would follow if you would let me use the barn chamber for a schoolroom of charitable purposes.

"You have read Hannah More's life," she went on. "You approve of her labors, I am certain, for the most degraded of England's paupers. Why not," she pleaded, "when it can be done without expense, let me teach some of the beggar children from the streets, who would otherwise remain untaught?"

Madame Dix acknowledged this note by saying that she had given the money to build the meetinghouse in Dixmount; that she donated a Bible for every newly married couple in the village; and that she proposed to have no beggar children, with their sores, running around in the yard at Dix Mansion.

Dorothea's brother Joseph, who was now finished with his work at Latin School, went into business in Dorchester. Her brother Charles Wesley, a strange, silent, and tormented boy, ran off to sea. The two women remained brooding in the house.

That autumn, as everyone had predicted, General Levi Lincoln of Worcester was elected Governor of Massachusetts, and he appointed Edward Bangs as Secretary of State.

Edward finally married a girl from Worcester much younger than he, and quite of the right family. Her name was Mary Grosvenor. The couple came to live in Boston in a house near the capitol on Beacon Hill.

At about this time Dorothea caught cold, and for some reason she did not stop coughing. Madame Dix watched her as she went about the house.

Finally, unable to stand it any longer, she cried, "Have your school for beggars then!"

Dorothea cleaned out the hayloft over the carriage house. The dust from the hay made her cough linger a little longer. She coughed slightly as she nailed up the sign on her school: "The Hope."

3

Under the Wheel

For five years Dorothea worked as if driven She rose at dawn. She went to bed at midnight. She wrote to her friend Ann, "There is so much to do, I am broken on a wheel."

She taught in a school for young ladies which she started in the house. She taught in her charity school in the loft of the carriage house. She wrote book after book for children, turning out eight books in five years. She tended the needs of beggar children, providing food, shoes, clothes.

She grew thin. Spots of fever burned in her cheeks. Dr. Channing told her one day in church, "A virtue carried to excess may also be a vice."

One day she crossed the yard to go to her charity school, The Hope. As she pulled open the heavy door of the carriage house, she felt a warm bubbling in her throat and she saw a crimson spot on her handkerchief. She shrugged her shoulders and went upstairs to teach.

Some weeks later she rose in the morning but fell back on her bed with a gush of blood from her throat. Dr. Hayward of the Massachusetts General Hospital came running. "Rheumatism of the lungs," he said gravely.

Dorothea lay ill for many weeks. Her grandmother sat by her bed recalling Dorothea's mistakes of the past—she should have accepted Edward Bangs; she should have married.

Dr. Channing and his wife came to see Dorothea. He confided how he himself had fallen ill in his youth; how kind friends, the William Rathbones of Liverpool, had nursed him back to health at their country estate, Greenbanks.

Madame Dix came into the room to complain once more about Dorothea's many mistakes. The old woman's nose, chin, and voice had grown sharper with age. Dorothea sighed wearily.

Dr. Channing and his wife exchanged a glance. They invited Dorothea to spend the summer with them at their country home, Oaklands, overlooking Narragansett Bay.

They needed a teacher, they said, for their two little daughters, who might otherwise forget during the summer what they had learned in the winter.

"But I am not well," said Dorothea.

"Then you will teach from the couch," Dr. Channing assured her.

Dorothea spent the summer with the Channings on the pleasant farm overlooking the ocean. White sails passed by the window.

Dr. Channing, coming into the parlor with his two little girls, often laughed. "What is that on the couch, a white cloud?"

"No," shouted the children, "Miss Dix!"

And soon Dorothea sat outside with them, or walked along the beach with them if the sun was not too hot, telling them stories.

That winter the Channings planned to spend at Saint Croix, one of the Virgin Islands, where he hoped to write a series of sermons showing that the problem of slavery could be solved without violence.

Mrs. Channing asked if Dorothea would care to go with them as a tutor for their children. Unable as yet to reopen her school at Dix Mansion, and dreading a solitary winter with her grandmother, Dorothea accepted with tears in her eyes.

"Happily!" she cried. "Happily!"

She loved the tiny minister. She loved his salty wife, who had put aside her fortune because Dr. Channing had refused to marry a rich woman. And Dorothea loved the two little girls who clamored for her stories.

In the autumn of 1830 Dorothea sailed with the Channings on the schooner *Rice Plant*, her grandmother objecting, of course, until the very last moment.

"You are better now. You should dress up and go out into society. At twenty-eight it is still possible to marry."

With this sound in her ears, Dorothea left. She returned six months later, rested, the wound in her lungs healed.

She opened both schools again, the boarding school in the house, the charity school in the loft. Her grandmother nagged her to marry. "Maybe Dr. Ezra Stiles Gannet," she suggested, "the pastoral assistant to Dr. Channing.

"Maybe Mr. Wentz, your French tutor, who has recently come into a little inheritance. Maybe a widower with children. . . .

"Maybe . . ."

Dorothea worked harder than ever before.

Five years later, in 1836, she had another complete collapse, an attack of bleeding from the lungs, which left her lying for weeks unable even to speak. She had to write her wishes on bits of paper. Madame Dix sat constantly by her bedside, talking, talking.

When Dorothea rose again, her body transparent, her voice only a whisper, Dr. Hayward advised her, "If you can get to Italy, it might save your life!"

She understood him. All dying consumptives went to Rome. Keats, the English poet, had perished there, writing "Here lies one whose name was writ in water."

"Anywhere! Anywhere!" she cried.

All day long her grandmother droned, "What? You will go and leave me alone?" On April 2, 1836, Dorothea sailed for Europe. She carried with her a letter of introduction to the Rathbones, at Greenbanks, near Liverpool.

Her plan was to land at Liverpool; travel on to London, rest there, and then make her way across the Continent to Rome, where Dr. Hayward hoped the bright Italian sunshine might restore her health.

She did not hope. Gaunt, wrapped in shawls, she watched the shore line drop away as the ship left New York. Then she went below to her cabin.

When the ship docked at Liverpool, she had no strength to go on. She lay ill for several days in a Liverpool hotel. Then she suffered another hemorrhage of the lungs. Before she became unconscious she scribbled a note to the Rathbones, at Greenbanks.

Sometime later she awoke in a high, bright room. From her window she could see a green, sloping lawn and a river.

She looked around. A woman in a gray Quaker gown sat near her. She had soft dark hair drawn down smoothly, like folded wings, about her face. She spoke gently.

"I am Mrs. Rathbone. We have brought thee to Greenbanks to get well."

Tears of weakness slipped from Dorothea's cheeks, and she slept. When she awoke, the woman was still there. She slept and awoke many times. Always the woman sat by her bedside.

For many months Dorothea lay ill at Greenbanks. Servants came and went by the door. Sometimes Mr. Rathbone, a kindly gentleman with sidewhiskers, looked in with his finger on his lips but did not speak.

The summer passed. The lawn grew dark. The river froze. And in the deep hush of winter, when icicles hung from the eaves, Dorothea's life seemed to flicker, a dying ember.

One day Mrs. Rathbone brought Dorothea a letter from America. "I hope this will not shock thee." It was a letter from Dr. Hayward's wife.

It told Dorothea gently that her grandmother had passed away at Dix Mansion. And in the same week, on a farm in New Hampshire, her mother had passed away too!

Dorothea began to sob. A cord of tension, passing through her body, seemed to break. To the doctor's amazement she began slowly to get better.

That spring she wrote to Ann in Brookline, "Today, for the first time I was able to walk about in my room." Several weeks later she sat on the lawn looking up at the strawberry Gothic mansion in which she had lain ill so long, and then at the River Mersey flowing between green banks toward the terrible slums of Liverpool.

When she grew better, Mr. Rathbone took her to see the slums, which as a humanitarian, and as mayor of Liverpool, he had tried to wipe out.

He showed her the stockades at the docks where once human beings were kept. Each year fifty thousand slaves had been shipped from Liverpool to America. And this traffic did not stop until America, breeding her own slaves, made the slave trade unprofitable.

Mr. Rathbone told her about the many families of Liverpool who had grown rich on this trade. Descended from such a family of shipowners, he gave away one half of his income each year to the poor.

"I do not enjoy my riches," he said. "We are judged by the way we let other human beings live."

In the gracious parlors at Greenbanks, Dorothea met zealous human beings working to ease suffering of every kind. She heard of little children chained to the loom in English factories, cutting threads and spinning bobbins sixteen hours a day, until their bodies grew twisted, and their legs grew shriveled so that, with their overgrown heads, they looked like little spiders, not children!

She heard of Englishwomen, with chains round their bodies, crawling on their hands and knees to draw coal through the darkest passages in the mines, where even the pit ponies would not go!

She met Lady Byron. She met the Earl of Shaftesbury, the fighting lord. And then one day she met a thin, gentle Quaker, Mr. Samuel Tuke, whose mild words shook her life so that she said bitterly, "Too late. Oh, too late!"

"It is never too late," he said quietly.

But she had no lungs; she had no health; she had no strength. She sat listening to him, brooding darkly while he told her the story of his family, which for three generations had worked to bring mercy to the mentally ill.

He told Dorothea how his grandfather William Tuke, a merchant of York, had been upset when a friend, a Quaker woman, died of a brutal beating in an asylum.

Gathering other Quaker friends around him, he raised money to buy a farm outside of York. And there he set up a refuge, The Retreat at York, where the Quaker brethren "when sick in their minds could be treated with loving-kindness."

Dorothea, listening, twisted her hands and thought of her father, whom no one had treated with loving-kindness, whom everyone had hated. All the heartbreak of her childhood came back. She could hardly hold back her tears.

"Do go on," she said to Samuel Tuke.

He told her that his grandfather did not know of another great man to whom had come the same wonderful thought of love for the mentally ill. This man, Pinel, a French doctor, struck the chains from the insane in the darkest dungeons of Bicêtre. One man had been in chains forty years. He embraced Pinel, and did not hurt him!

Samuel Tuke told Dorothea about The Retreat at York, where he worked, now, as his father and his grandfather had worked before him.

He told her about this place of sunny rooms, and pleasant gardens, where the sick were provided with books to read, and music to soothe them, "and gentle, loving servants to tend them."

"Just because a person may be insane upon one subject," he pleaded, "does not necessarily mean that he will be insensible to human kindness."

He told her that no human being in God's sight could ever be too repulsive to love. "And should we then shut any human beings from our sight and from our love?"

He told her indignantly how the insane were displayed at old Bedlam for a fee, families coming on Sundays to watch them at their antics.

He told her of insane people who were set on the road to beg and to starve, or were tied in chains in cellars and attics, their cries for mercy unheard, "because we think they are insane and they do not feel!"

He went on to tell Dorothea that "the mentally sick are imprisoned in their sickness, and they above all need our kindness and our love to help them."

Tears dropped down on her hands as she twisted them, murmuring, "Too late, too late."

Samuel Tuke left her. "I hope we shall meet again. I do not often meet those to whom I can talk so freely from my heart."

He gave her two books, a translation of the writings of Pinel, whom he called the "great liberator," and a small volume he had written about loving care for the mentally sick.

She carried these books in her portmanteau when

14,542

she returned to America in the autumn of 1837. She was thirty-five years old. She had only one lung.

She closed the big house on Orange Court, where her grandmother's voice seemed still to echo. She wandered through the empty rooms for the last time, thinking of the news which had been brought to her on shipboard.

Her cousin Edward had passed away while still serving as Secretary of State. He had never become Governor; nor she a governor's wife, nor anything else. Of what use could she be to the world?

It seemed to her that for the last time she could hear her grandmother's stick on the stairs, and her bitter voice saying, "You have ruined your life."

Dorothea sighed, closed the door of Dix Mansion, and went down the walk. She had been forbidden to stay in Boston during the cold weather. She began the life of a wandering invalid.

She went south to Virginia in the winter. She stayed in a boardinghouse in Boston during the summer. She dropped away from all of her old friends except Ann.

She wrote her one day, "It is terrible to live like this, neither hot nor cold." She haunted libraries. She read a little about the treatment of the insane. A few private hospitals, copying the methods of the Retreat at York, had been started in America—the McLean Hospital in Boston, and the Hartford Retreat.

Then Horace Mann, a legislator in the Massachusetts Assembly, somehow secured the money to open a small state hospital in Worcester. Dr. Samuel Woodward, trained at the Hartford Retreat in the methods of Samuel Tuke, came to manage this hospital, which immediately became overcrowded and stopped taking more patients.

All this Dorothea heard as someone traveling in a coach might see distant trees whiz by, or a vista of a house in a clearing which for a moment would haunt her and then disappear.

In the winter of 1841, growing very restless, despite the doctor's orders, Dorothea returned to Boston before the snow had disappeared from the ground.

On a day of March slush and wind she went gloomily to the nearest church to hear a sermon. The preacher, Dr. Lowell, spoke well, but for some reason she could not fix her thoughts for even a moment on what he was saying.

As she left the church, holding her umbrella against the wind and clutching her shawl, she heard some men behind her talking about the terrible condition of the insane poor held in dark caverns beneath the East Cambridge Jail.

She turned around; but the wind tore at her umbrella, threatening to turn it inside out, her shawl slipped from her shoulders, and other people intervened between her and the men who had spoken.

She returned to her room, where she sat for some days darkly brooding. The snow and slush did not disappear but dripped gloomily past her window.

One day the landlady called to her, "You have a caller, Miss Dix."

She started up in surprise. A young man came in and timidly begged her pardon for his dripping greatcoat and his equally dripping beaver, which immediately made a puddle on the floor.

She recognized John Nichols, a thin, earnest youth, the son of a woman she had known when she taught at Dix Mansion.

He told her he was now studying for the ministry at Harvard, and that, advised by his mother, he had come to seek her help.

"My help?" she said sternly. "How can I help anyone?"

He told her that, as part of his work, he had been obliged to teach the Bible to a group of women in jail. But he had been unable to hold their interest.

'If only you could help me!" He leaned forward flushing. "If only you knew of some kind woman who would be willing to go to the jail for a few Sundays, to teach for me! Maybe she could win their attention. Maybe she could hold their interest."

"Some woman?" she cried. "Where is the jail?"

"Only across the river," he answered, startled. "It's not far."

"Where is it? Where is it?" She gripped the arms of her chair. "Tell me the name of the jail!"

He looked at her amazed. "It's the Middlesex County House of Correction. Most people call it the East Cambridge Jail."

Her knuckles on the chair grew white. "I will go there myself."

"Miss Dix"—he jumped up—"I could never permit that. My mother has told me about your delicate health!"

She picked up his damp hat from the floor and handed it to him sternly. "I will be there next Sunday."

4

Lamp in the Dark

The following Sunday, in the snow and slush, Dorothea went to East Cambridge. The jail lay in a region of swamps. The corridors smelled of damp, stale mutton and human misery.

Dorothea taught a dozen sullen women in a high, bare cell, and the light fell in stripes on her Bible. When the women filed out she turned to the jailer, a big beefy man with puffy eyelids.

"Show me where your insane are kept!"

He objected. "No one goes down there!" But finally he took her past the rows of cells looking down upon the gallows; past the terrible scaffold; and then out into the prison yard, where he lifted up a heavy trap door at the edge of one of the buildings.

She followed him down moldy steps into a black cavern filled with the chill of the swamps. He lit a lantern and she saw what at first she took to be a part of the foundations, a thick pier of stone which ran the full length of the cavern. Then she perceived at either side of the structure a row of black, rusty iron doors.

She shrank. "Not in there?"

The jailer explained that in the cells once used for the solitary confinement of murderous prisoners the county now kept its indigent insane.

"No one can hear them down here."

He opened door after door for her. Her senses could not take in the screams and the smells. But as he held up the lantern in the dark, she saw what she was never to forget—emaciated human beings on filthy straw in rags and in chains!

She saw two women penned side by side in coops made of slats. One woman was old and toothless, her white hair streaming, and she screamed furiously.

Dorothea knelt down beside her. She gently touched her bony shoulder. Fierce eyes, burning with suspicion, turned on her. Then suddenly the woman wept.

In this moment of silence Dorothea turned to the other cage in which a young girl sat, her clothes torn to shreds. Shivering, she said to Dorothea, "I'm cold."

Dorothea tore off her shawl and was about to put it around the trembling girl, but the jailer pulled her from the cell and hastily closed the black iron door.

Later Dorothea found herself in the yard. As the jailer stamped heavily on the trap door, she whirled on him with fury.

"Why don't you put a stove down there?"

He shrugged. "There hasn't been a stove down there since the jail was built."

"But couldn't you see how the damp ran from the walls?"

"Nonsense." He led her out through the prison. "Those people down there are insane. They cannot feel the cold like you or I."

She stood by the prison gate arguing. The jailer became impatient. "That's not up to me; it's up to the county commissioners."

The next morning Dorothea returned to East Cambridge. She pulled open the heavy door of the county courthouse situated not far from the jail. She found the hallway blue with smoke and crowded with arguing politicians who looked at her contemptuously.

She asked a red-necked man, "Where can I find the county commissioners?"

He spat tobacco juice and jerked his thumb. "Over there in *general sessions.*"

She squeezed into a room crowded with politicians who were arguing for contracts to supply the jail and the poorhouse with tallow, mutton, and coal. "We give 'em the votes; they gotta give us the contracts," she heard.

She pushed her way to the rail. Behind it, poised like angry hornets, sat three men, all lean, all bald, all looking as if they would sting if another human being spoke to them.

She put her hands on the rail. "Gentlemen, I want to request that a stove be put into the basement of the East Cambridge Jail to warm the indigent insane, who are freezing there."

"What?" screamed the commissioner nearest her.

She repeated her request.

"No personal petitions today!"

"I am not speaking for myself. I am speaking for mankind!"

A roar of laughter filled the room.

She went home. She returned the next day, and the day after that, and her black cloak and bonnet became a familiar symbol.

The chief commissioner, wearied, anxious to get rid of her, finally said, "We'll appoint a committee to investigate."

She came back again, day after day. "The jail lies only across the way," she pleaded. "It should take scarcely ten minutes to go there and come back and make a report."

Someone laughed. "What a life this would be if women got into politics! It's a good thing they can't vote."

"Vote?" A guffaw went up in the room.

Six weeks later, a committee having duly investigated, they gave a report. Someday when the county had more money a bigger jail should be built.

"But the stove!" shouted Dorothea from the back of the room, for they had not let her get near to the rail this time.

"The stove!"

"Committee report approved," rapped the chief commissioner. "No further petitions will be received until action has been taken on this report."

"But until you build a new jail!"

The commissioner rapped again.

"No action!"

In despair, knowing he had recently been ill, Dorothea went to her old friend Dr. Channing in his home on Mt. Vernon Street, near the state capitol.

As she climbed the steep street, on the side of Beacon Hill, she saw the golden dome of the State House glittering above her.

Below her she could see the river. And beyond the river lay the swamps which had been filled when the East Cambridge Jail was built.

She stood before Dr. Channing in his study. She told him the story of the East Cambridge Jail. She told him the story of the jailer. She told him the story of the county commissioners.

She did not weep, for she had gone far beyond tears. But, twisting her hands, she asked the tiny minister, as a child might ask God, "How can people be so cruel, so inhuman?"

"Not cruel," he told her mildly, "only dull."

She gazed at him, and in this way she was always to remember him, his small face illumined and shining like a star against the dark books.

"Not all have your capacity to feel human suffering," he told her quietly. "Do not be impatient. Know that those who do not understand you, can be educated."

"The jailer? The county commissioners?" Her lips felt dry. "How?"

He suggested that she rouse public opinion, and gave her the names of three of his parishioners who knew how to do this: Horace Mann, Charles Sumner, Dr. Samuel Gridley Howe.

"Some people call them the three horsemen of reform."

She went to call, first, on Dr. Samuel Gridley Howe at the Perkins Institute for the Blind, housed now in a converted hotel in South Boston.

She found him with Laura Bridgman, a blind, deaf, and mute child, beside him. The little girl held up her palms with fingers outstretched as Dorothea entered.

"She hears and she sees and she speaks with her fingers," said Dr. Howe, a frail, bearded man of strange, gentle force. "Before, she lived in darkness."

"I know of others who live in greater darkness!" Dorothea cried.

He looked surprised.

She did not sit down but remained standing as she talked, clutching her shawl. Once it fell to the floor, and Laura Bridgman, smiling, picked it up. Dr. Howe did not fail to note this gesture, and touched the child tenderly. She put her head against his chest, and stayed there as if listening, while Dorothea went on talking. The words poured from her, almost wildly.

"Dr. Howe, I know that you are busy. I know that you have recently appeared before the legislatures in seventeen states to plead the cause of the blind.

"I know that you ran for and were recently elected to our state legislature here in Massachusetts because you need help for your school.

"I know that you believe every blind child should be a ward of the state, and you are giving every waking hour and every ounce of your strength to this great cause.

"Nobody should divert you, Dr. Howe, any more than they should divert Horace Mann in his great fight for public education, or Charles Sumner in his great fight against slavery."

She broke off and leaned toward him, holding the edge of his desk with her fingers. "I would not come to you or to them if I could help it.

"If I only knew what you knew, I would do the work that is needed myself. But I don't even know how to begin, Dr. Howe, and you must show me."

She told him of the horrors she had seen, of her failures with the jailer of the East Cambridge prison, and of her still greater failure with the county commissioners.

"I don't know how to talk yet. I don't know how to make myself understood. I don't know how to move public opinion."

"I will help you," said Dr. Howe.

The little girl, still pressing her head against his heart, gave a radiant smile. Then she came round the table and very lightly, with mothlike fingers, felt Dorothea's face.

Dorothea was never to forget this touch.

Some weeks later an article appeared in the *Boston Advertiser* written by Dr. Samuel Gridley Howe. It told of Dorothea's visit to him. It told of his own visit to the East Cambridge Jail. It told of the sufferings he had seen, "not fit for our time."

Dorothea felt jubilant.

But the next day and the next day, stunned, she read the *Boston Advertiser.* There were whole columns of denial from the county commissioners in East Cambridge.

"Lies! Slander!" they cried. Miss Dix, a hysterical spinster, had bedeviled and fooled the all-to-generous Dr. Howe.

"No such conditions exist in the East Cambridge Jail."

Dorothea ran to Dr. Howe. To her amazement she found him happy. "We have drawn blood!" he cried. "Now everyone will be interested in the East Cambridge Jail."

Dorothea walked home wondering. Was this the way to arouse public opinion? She trembled with rage. She could have torn the county commissioners to pieces.

Everyone in Boston respected Charles Sumner, the beetle-browed orator whose lyceums against slavery had stirred thousands. She went to see him in his office at Harvard, where he lectured on jurisprudence.

"Howe has spoken to me," he said. "I will do what I can."

On September 8, 1841, there appeared in the *Boston Advertiser* a letter written by Charles Sumner to Dr. Samuel Gridley Howe.

"My dear Howe," it said. "All that was reported of the East Cambridge Jail is true. I have been there. I have seen all that you have seen. Let me write of one case."

He told of the two women in coops, "one furiously mad, screaming vilest imprecations all day; the other slightly melancholy, her reason scarcely clouded.

"In this way," the letter went on, "in heathen times, the dead were sometimes tied to the living, the cruelest of punishments. Such horrors I saw in the East Cambridge Jail!"

People read and were shocked. New letters flooded the columns of the *Boston Advertiser*—letters of protest against such conditions.

The county commissioners voted hastily to install a stove in the basement of the East Cambridge Jail, to give warmth "to the insane housed now in the cells of solitary confinement."

Dorothea's mind leaped forward. Why should the insane be in prison at all? She went to see Horace Mann, the head of the State Board of Education.

Tall, radiant, with prematurely white hair which made his dark eyes look darker, he greeted her. "I have heard of your work, Miss Dix."

"Why don't we have a bigger hospital in Worcester?" she asked.

"Money."

"Why won't the state legislature vote the money?"

"They say there is no need."

"There is no need? Why, the need could be shown."

"How?"

"A survey could be made."

Horace Mann gave a bitter laugh. "They won't vote the money for a survey. They say there is no need for a survey."

"Ah"—she put her finger to her lips—"the commissioners in East Cambridge!" She rose from the chair. "Then we must educate the legislature. We must convince them."

"How?" He now watched her.

She turned to him, and her face lit up as if she had found the answer.

"Quite simply," she said, "a private person must make that survey at his own cost."

Horace Mann shook his head at her naïveté. "Miss Dix!" He went to the wall and pulled down a huge map of Massachusetts, colored pink, blue, and yellow, with all the mountains and waterways marked, and all the towns indicated.

"Miss Dix, are you acquainted with our state? Do you see how it stretches in vast territory from the

Hoosac Mountains, in the west, to the tip of Cape Cod, far out in the Atlantic Ocean?

"Do you know there are over five hundred towns, villages, and hamlets in this state by the last census; that many of them cannot be reached by coach, rail, canal, and some not even by a rough country wagon?

"Do you know what it would mean to visit every town, village, and hamlet in the state? Do you know what it would mean to talk to the village selectmen who hate intrusion, and then to the almshouse keepers and the overseers of the poor who would grudge any visits to their institutions?

"Do you know what it would mean to visit every jail, workhouse, and almshouse in the state where an insane person might be held in durance?

"Do you know what it would mean to document every case of human suffering in the state? Facts, Miss Dix—only facts would convince the legislature."

He turned to her. "Can you think of any man in his right mind who would undertake such a survey?"

She stood for a moment, head bowed. Then with a deep sigh she answered him, her eyes slowly meeting his. "I did not say a man."

He gazed at her.

"A woman might."

"Miss Dix!"

She spoke to him that afternoon, as she had never

spoken to any other human being, of her feeling for the mentally tormented whom no one else loved.

A few days later she left to start her survey.

5

The White Towns

The lovely white towns of Massachusetts, serene with gleaming white dwellings and shining white church spires, seemed to show no sign of suffering.

Dorothea went from town to town. Everywhere she discovered the furtive road which led to the poorhouse. And behind the poorhouse, in barns, shed, and stalls, she found the indigent insane.

In Dedham, where Horace Mann once had practiced law, and where he first had dreamed of helping the mentally sick, she found a penned woman who seemed to be quite in her right mind. She was tied in a dark stall behind the almshouse. No one could remember why she had been put there. No one seemed to care that she should be released.

Dorothea went to plead with the overseer of the poor in the big, new, expensive county courthouse. "Send this woman to Worcester to be tested," she begged. "It will cost only a few dollars!"

"We can't waste county money!"

In Danvers, not far from Boston, Dorothea found a girl in a barn, in a coop made of slats, on a pile of filth, her body streaming sores.

"Why don't you make this poor girl a bed of clean straw," Dorothea begged of the keeper, a woman, "and put some fresh garments on her?"

The keeper replied sullenly, "Of what use would it be? She wouldn't know the difference."

In Shelburne, on the Connecticut River, toward the western part of the state, Dorothea discovered a man in a cage being fed like an animal, his food thrown to him on the floor.

"Why don't you give him a plate?" she protested.

"It's all the same to him how he eats," grunted the keeper.

In another town, which she visited in the spring, she saw a young man peering wistfully from the door of a little shed by the edge of the road; his neck was bound by an iron collar attached by a chain to the wall. The collar had worn a huge sore in his neck.

She asked the keeper, "Why don't you take off that collar?"

He spat with authority on the dust of the road and drawled, to correct her, "He likes that collar."

"He likes that collar?"

"Why, ma'am, I had a cousin up Vermont way, crazy as a wildcat he was. So I got me a blacksmith to make him a collar out of a good solid piece of iron. I put that collar on the boy, and believe me, ma'am, he liked it."

"He liked it? How do you know?"

The keeper spat again, arching tobacco juice through two missing teeth under a stained, ragged mustache.

"Why, he never tried to run away again, ma'am, He stayed put, just as happy as could be!"

Dorothea went away stunned.

In Newton, not far from Boston, she found the worst case of suffering she had ever seen—in a crib filled with straw, an old man tied with chains; and from the straw protruded not legs, but stumps.

The keeper explained to her that the old man had been "farmed out" by the town, and the farmer who kept him had forgotten him one night in a shed that was freezing cold.

The old man's feet froze off and he was returned to the care of the town, where he had been since held in a barn behind the almshouse.

"But why do you keep him chained?" Dorothea asked.

"Oh, he might crawl and do some damage," the woman keeper answered. The old man lay asleep, his long hair and beard mingled with the straw, his features hardly visible.

"Would you like to see him better?" the keeper offered. "Here, I'll get a stick and I'll stir him up."

"No, no!" Dorothea cried, hardly holding back her tears. "If sleep can visit a wretch so forlorn, how merciless it would be to break his slumber."

In her notebook Dorothea wrote wearily that night, "The keepers have to be educated. Familiarity with suffering may blunt sensibilities. Where neglect once takes a footing other injuries are multiplied."

At the end of a year and a half Dorothea returned to Boston, her portmanteau heavy with many black notebooks. She had visited almost five hundred towns. She had recorded the sufferings of a thousand insane.

She had traveled by train, coach, wagon; by swaying canal boat. She had slept in taverns and farmhouses, on boats and trains, sometimes not even separated by a curtain from the rough men passengers.

She had endured the contempt of village selectmen and county overseers of the poor. She had been called a "meddlesome busybody" and a "nosy spinster." She had ranged the villages of the Monadnocks; the fishing towns of Cape Cod and the whaling towns of the southern harbors, haunted always by the vision of white sails.

Everywhere she had found the same inhumanity, the same indifference to human suffering. Everywhere she had to fight her streaming love for the most unfortunate of mankind, gathering facts and serving no one case in need; for in serving all she knew she would in the end serve each one of them. But she knew the cases of horror she had seen would never be removed from her memory.

She said to herself constantly, "I must learn how to be temperate." She fought continually to still the torment in her breast.

She had written in her notebooks only the barest of facts. She wanted never to write a word of emotion again—only facts.

"It would be too much," she said with trembling lips. It would be too much to open the door; to reveal the tumults of her mind, the centuries she had lived since leaving Boston.

She returned to the Channing home on Mt. Vernon

Street, within sight of the State House with its shining golden dome.

Mrs. Channing, in widow's weeds, met her at the door. Both women wept. Dr. Channing had passed away the winter before. He lay buried at Mt. Auburn Cemetery in Cambridge, under a huge pine tree scarred by storms.

In Dr. Channing's study, by a window from which the distant bulk of the State House could be seen, Dorothea began her *Memorial to the Massachusetts Legislature,* asking for funds to build a large state hospital in Worcester.

She wrote only facts, a ledger of inhumanity, terse items to stab the conscience, page upon page upon page, naming town after town and case after case.

Lincoln: a woman caged.

Franklin: a man in chains.

Taunton: a woman in a cage.

Medford: a man in a stall for seventeen years.

Newton: a man without legs, chained.

But finally the intense emotion which Dorothea had held back so long, rushed out on paper. "Gentlemen of Massachusetts," she wrote, "I come to present to you the strong claims of suffering humanity. I come as the advocate of the helpless, forgotten, insane men and women held in cages, closets, cellars, stalls, pens; chained, naked, beaten with rods, lashed.

"Gentlemen," she pleaded, remembering her heartbreak with the county commissioners in East Cambridge and fearing she would not be heard, "I beg, I implore you to put away the spirit of selfishness and self-seeking. Lay off the armor of local strife and political ambition.

"Forget, I beg you, the earthly and perishable, the thought without mercy. Gentlemen, I commit you to a sacred cause!"

She read this *Memorial,* when it was finished late in December, 1842, to Horace Mann, Dr. Samuel Gridley Howe, Dr. Samuel Woodward, Charles Sumner, and Dr. Luther V. Bell of the McLean Hospital—all gathered in Mrs. Channing's living room.

Horace Mann jumped up. "I feel as I used to in my youth, that no human being should die until he has achieved some victory for humanity." He embraced Dorothea.

With a tremor she had not felt when Edward Bangs held her, Dorothea disengaged herself from Horace Mann's embrace, her eyes brimming with tears.

Dr. Howe said, "The legislature convenes in January. I will introduce your measure in the House. At least two hundred thousand dollars will be needed to build an addition to the Worcester State Hospital. I will ask for that sum."

"I will help," offered Charles Sumner.

"I shall advise," said Horace Mann, who had served fourteen years in House and Senate—part of the time as president of the Senate—before becoming head of the newly formed State Board of Education.

"When the time comes we will give facts," offered Dr. Samuel Woodward, the kindly, bearded head of the Worcester State Hospital, which had been overcrowded for almost ten years.

"And I will do all I can," said Dr. Luther Bell, who had quite some time ago founded a hospital in Boston, after the manner of the Retreat at York, where people of means, though mentally tormented, could be treated with kindness.

"Then, kind friends," said Dorothea, "it lies in your hands. My part of the work is done."

"Your work is nobly done, but not yet ended!" Dr. Samuel Gridley Howe told her in a worried note several days later.

The House had convened. "I presented your *Memorial,*" he wrote on a bitter cold day in January, "both as a memorial and as a petition."

He had presented the *Memorial,* he confided, to a House consisting of country lawyers and small businessmen, dedicated to keeping their seats, by showing the taxpayers that they could rule prudently—without new expenditures that would raise taxes.

"I have touched off the piece," Dr. Howe told Dorothea. "But you will have to furnish the ammunition. Select some newspaper as your cannon," he urged, "and discharge red-hot shot into the hearts of the people, so that they shall warm up the clams and oysters of the House to deeds of charity."

Mrs. Channing stood with knitting needles clicking as Dorothea read this note.

"Who opposes you?"

"Three hundred commissioners from East Cambridge," said Dorothea cryptically.

She wrote articles to the newspapers. She described graphically what she had seen in Danvers, Groton, Wayland, Westford, Sudbury, Shelburne, and other towns near and far from Boston.

She sent these articles to the *Boston Advertiser* and to the *Boston Courier,* which at first gladly printed her accounts and then refused.

The people of Danvers had drawn up a counter-memorial saying her facts were not true. The *Greenfield Gazette,* upstate, said she had written lies about the town of Shelburne.

The *Boston Courier,* once friendly to her, now wrote of her *Memorial* before the legislature that "the public would be *quite* liberal if they discounted her facts at fifty per cent."

Horace Mann came to advise her. "Such assertions must be fought."

Dr. Samuel Gridley Howe told her that in the legislature "men without hearts" had determined "to kill that hospital bill at all costs."

"How can you prove your facts again?" said Horace Mann. "How can you breach the walls of inhumanity?"

"I know!" she cried. "The third horseman!"

She went to see Charles Sumner at Harvard, where he sat frowning over a speech against slavery. "Ah," he said, "if words could only be bullets!"

"Mr. Sumner"—she interrupted his thoughts so rudely his dark eyes glared at her for a moment as though she were an enemy to be destroyed with the baleful glare—"Mr. Sumner, you must take time to help me again."

She had brought with her a copy of her *Memorial to the Massachusetts Legislature*. She opened it to page nineteen, ruffling the pages over the manuscript of his speech.

"Here on page nineteen," she breathed on his shoulder, "are some facts relating to four towns, all lying within a few miles of Boston.

"Visit these towns, Mr. Sumner, attest what you have seen. Only go, see, and tell what exists in Sudbury, Groton, Westford, and Wayland, as you did once before about East Cambridge."

"Ah, Miss Dix"—he pushed away his speech and

took up her papers—"we should have such fighters as you for the cause of abolition."

"Our cause chooses us." . . .

He went, though the roads in mid-February lay frozen. He told Dorothea, "For you I have earned chilblains and a cold in my chest."

"But for humanity?"

"Ah, humanity, Miss Dix! Humanity!" he sighed.

Some days later a terse account appeared in the *Boston Courier*—a personal statement by Charles Sumner, whom all in Boston admired.

"I read over very carefully the account that Miss Dix had given in her *Memorial* of conditions existing in the almshouses in Sudbury, Wayland, Westford, and Groton.

"I went in person to these places to check the truth of the facts stated. I am obliged to state these facts untrue *only* to this extent, that neither her words nor mine can convey an adequate picture of the sufferings to be seen in these places. In the name of humanity I urge immediate passage of her bill now before the Massachusetts legislature."

Letters asking passage of the hospital bill now poured into the newspapers. In the legislature, men began to think of some way to kill the bill by technicalities. All kinds of delaying tactics were interposed by enemies of the bill.

Horace Mann, able and experienced in spite of his radiant idealism, advised Dr. Samuel Gridley Howe in advance how to meet every delaying tactic.

On February 22, Dr. Howe rose to remind members of the legislature of the prudence for which Massachusetts is famous—rose under the massive stuffed cod which hangs in the House. Bones of that cod fertilize the bogs where grow the cranberries which grace the table of plenty on Thanksgiving—a table spread through prior prudence.

"Gentlemen," he appealed to the canny lawyers and storekeepers eying him with the dour suspicion that his speech would raise taxes, "Gentlemen, I move for resolves on the hospital bill. I move we vote two hundred thousand dollars to build an addition to the state hospital for the insane at Worcester."

Gray of Boston jumped up, tense and blue of lip. "I oppose that motion on the general ground that the orders of the day ought not to be disturbed!"

Dr. Howe ignored this technicality. "Two hundred applications to the state hospital are rejected each year for lack of room. A thousand insane lie in attics and cellars!"

Dr. Jarvis rose. "Is Massachusetts too poor to do her duty?"

On the following evening Dorothea received a message from Dr. Howe. "Your bill has passed!"

That night the house on Mt. Vernon Street filled with jubilant visitors. Mr. Sumner came; Dr. Woodward, Dr. Bell, Dr. Samuel Gridley Howe almost beside himself with exhaustion and excitement.

"Wait!" he cried. "Wait until Miss Ward hears of this!"

Everyone knew he referred to Julia Ward, a poetess from New York, a young and beautiful girl, the daughter of a banker, with whom at the age of forty-three he had fallen in love.

Horace Mann finally appeared in the doorway, tall and radiant. He grasped Dorothea by the wrists. Impulsively he pressed his cheek to hers.

In the excitement, the intoxication of this wonderful hour, Dorothea glowed as she never had in her girlhood when Edward Bangs embraced her.

"You have won a victory for humanity!" Horace Mann cried.

When all the guests had gone, Dorothea, her cheeks and lips burning, sat down and impulsively penned a letter to the radiant human being, the first she had known in all her life who seemed to understand her.

This letter exists today. "Dear friend," she wrote to Horace Mann, "in all my efforts to help the suffering, I have only followed in the footpaths you have trodden."

She went on to speak of his achievement in having

broken the way for suffering humanity by creating the Worcester State Hospital, to which her own present efforts would only add.

She spoke of his great achievement for free education—the building of normal schools to train teachers; the creation of schools to teach poor and rich alike, an effort she had feebly attempted at Orange Court.

She tried to show him that he was greater than she. "I know that the usages of society crush free and cordial friendship, and silence the expression of actual truehearted sympathy," she admitted sadly.

"And to reveal the united sentiments of the heart and mind," she went on, "is almost as infrequent as to find hearts to cherish and minds to enshrine."

She leaned against the table as she wrote, and she could feel the echoing sound of her heart. She hesitated, trying to calm herself.

Then impetuously she put down the final words, which she was to regret all her life. "I shall think of you as one of the very few upon whose image my thoughts can repose with no distrust, and who are garnered to my heart with the most sacred affection."

No response came to this letter. What response could come? A few days later she heard that Horace Mann and Mary Peabody, to whom he had been secretly engaged, planned to be married at the same time as Dr. Samuel Gridley Howe and Julia Ward;

that all four planned to go to Europe for a joint honeymoon.

Dorothea packed her portmanteau.

"Where are you going?" asked Mrs. Channing.

"To Rhode Island," replied Dorothea. "I have received a letter from a clergyman, Dr. Edward Hall, who asks me to investigate a case of most dire suffering."

She took the Worcester railroad, which had been built through Horace Mann's legislative efforts. As the train drew away, a long plume of smoke floated over the valley and then disappeared.

And so disappeared the belated reawakening of her youth. She began to plan how she might help the cause of the mentally tormented in Rhode Island.

She got off in Providence with deep lines on her face and yet somehow feeling stronger, like someone with a fever who starts suddenly to recover.

"Where can I find Dr. Hall?" she asked.

6

Poor Simmons

In the darkening study of his parsonage Dorothea listened to Dr. Hall talking earnestly. He poked the fire against the February wind which crept in at the windows, then turned to her the face of one who strives greatly with small powers.

"We have in Rhode Island a case of dire suffering which can only be corrected if a rich man is awakened to conscience."

She looked at him puzzled. "What do you mean, Dr. Hall?"

"We have here in Rhode Island an insane man whose condition I shall not describe to you.

"This man could be sent to a hospital for proper care, but we have, by order of the General Assembly, only half a hospital."

Dorothea leaned forward. "I don't understand you, Dr. Hall."

"You soon shall, Miss Dix; you soon shall."

Dr. Hall rose. It had grown dark now in the shabby room filled with books. He lit a lamp. In the white glow his thin face, crowned with strands of thin dark hair, looked worried and strained as if he had long been fighting some great ordeal.

"I know I should not interest myself in such matters, but I cannot help it," he admitted. "Suffering of any kind moves me deeply, deeply."

"I quite understand," said Dorothea.

"Sometime ago," he said, "a rich merchant died in Providence. His name was Nicholas Brown. He had founded Brown University. He bequeathed thirty thousand dollars for the building of a humane retreat for the insane."

"Well," said Dorothea. She sat forward, eagerly.

"Not so fast, not so fast," warned Dr. Hall, and he sighed. "Mr. Nicholas Brown, a most canny businessman, left his money on condition."

"Well?" said Dorothea.

"That his money could not be used until some single person equaled the sum of his contribution, and then the hospital could be named in honor of that person."

He paused for a moment lost in thought.

"Do go on," said Dorothea.

"In all of Providence we have only one man who could easily part with such a sum. And he will not do it. And so, although our hospital is already chartered, it cannot be built!"

"Who is this man?" asked Dorothea.

"An aged bachelor, a man of great wealth, who keeps himself locked in a gloomy mansion, attended by a servant whose task it is to keep away all supplicants for charity."

"Who is this man?"

"Cyrus Butler."

"Cyrus Butler?"

"Yes, the owner of vast fleets engaged in the China trade. His fortune is fabulous."

"Have you approached him?"

"Yes, once with the members of a committee."

"What happened?"

"We found him hard as flint, not to be moved." The minister looked at his hands, which quivered a little. "He put us out of the house."

"Did he ever give to any charity in Providence?" Dorothea thoughtfully asked.

The minister shook his head. "Moses could more easily strike water from a rock."

Dorothea looked at the minister. "What do you want with me?" she asked.

"We thought," ventured Dr. Hall, "that from your experience you might know of some way to reach such a man."

"I know of no way," she told him, "except to lay before him the most pitiful case of human suffering we can find."

"We have such a case," said the minister in a low voice. His hands again seemed to tremble. "It is the case of dire suffering about which I wrote you—poor Simmons, in Little Compton. But I could not ask you to go there."

"Why?" She knit her brows and studied him; for he seemed to turn quite pale, perspiration showing on his forehead. He wiped his brow, with hands trembling still more violently.

"I have not slept since I went."

"Then I shall go tomorrow!" Dorothea told him. And the next day she took the coach to Little Compton, a village far out on Narragansett Bay, on a point of land swept by cold winds from the sea.

She fought her way across the Green and down a shabby road to the almshouse, a bleak dwelling which lay, as usual, beyond the town.

She found the almshousekeeper in a steaming kitchen filled with fetid smells, but it was a welcome warmth after the cold February wind which had torn at her back.

"May I see poor Simmons?" Dorothea asked.

The keeper sucked toothless gums. "Then keep your shawl on, for the wind out there can cut you to the bone. The swamps at this time of the year are still quite frozen."

Dorothea followed her through a rutted yard, past some broken-down barns and outhouses, to a swampy field of frozen black mud.

There she saw what seemed to be a tomb sticking up out of the ground. Drawing nearer, she saw that it was a structure of stone and that, at the side, some steps had been hollowed out which led to a door half-submerged in the ground and tied with a huge iron chain.

The almshousekeeper took out a key for the padlock which hung on the door.

"Now stand back," she warned as she turned the rusty key with an effort. "He may be behind the door, and he is furiously mad. Though he's chained, he can kill you."

Dorothea pushed open the door in spite of the keeper's warning.

"Do take care. Don't go inside, I tell you. Peep from the door."

She found herself in a chamber made of rocks,

so low she had to bend her head. At first she could see nothing. But she heard a chain move, and near her she felt someone breathing.

Then her eyes became accustomed to the gray half-light which fell from the partially opened door. Standing against the wall, in chains, she saw what at first she took to be a corpse.

She saw a man all bone, his skin a ghastly color as if mildewed. White tangled hair fell to his shoulders. Rags without color clung to his body.

He stood barefoot in mud, a chain with a heavy bar attached to his leg; and from this bar another chain was attached to the rock in the ceiling.

He stood without moving, his head stooped because the cell was too low. He stood silent, looking at her with eyes as from the grave.

She put her arms around him. Her shoulders shook. He wept. Their tears mingled. . . .

When she came out, the keeper said in amazement, "He did not hurt you!"

Dorothea, averting her face, asked, "How long has he been down there?"

"Three years."

Dorothea said no more.

She returned to Providence. She wrote an article for the *Providence Journal*—an article about her visit to poor Simmons.

"There he stood," she wrote, "in darkness, encased on every side by walls of frost, with only wet straw to lie upon and a sheet of ice for his cover.

"No doubt," she went on, "the people of Rhode Island profess to worship. Do they pray, I wonder, to the same God who looks down on poor Simmons?"

This article appeared on April 10, 1844, and brought, as usual, furious denials, and the suggestion that "Miss Dix, quite obviously a meddlesome person, should go back to Massachusetts. Her facts are untrue!"

As Dorothea had once asked Charles Sumner to check her facts in Massachusetts, she now asked Mr. Thomas G. Hazard, the State Commissioner of the Poor for Rhode Island, to make a visit to poor Simmons.

He did so, and wrote in the *Providence Journal,* "I can attest that Miss Dix is no troublemonger. She has ferreted out some cases of human suffering beyond belief.

"The case of poor Simmons, to which I was yesterday an eyewitness, goes beyond anything I supposed to exist in the civilized world!"

Dorothea sent copies of her article, the letters of denunciation, and the letter of approval to Mr. Cyrus Butler in his gloomy mansion. Then she said to Dr. Hall, "The time has come to call on Mr. Butler."

"I shall go with you only to the door," said the Reverend Mr. Hall. "My courage would carry me no further."

She climbed the stairs of the dark stone mansion covered on all sides with ivy. She raised the huge iron doorknocker, heard its distant echoes, and tried to calm herself by thinking of poor Simmons.

The door creaked. A sour manservant looked at her suspiciously. She told him who she was. He left her standing and went down the hall.

After a long time he returned and led her into a huge room crowded drearily with massive dark furniture. In the depths of a mammoth brown chair she saw a little old man with a face wrinkled like a walnut.

He lifted withered lids to look at her with steel-sharp eyes. "What do you want?" he asked curtly.

"The courtesy of a chair," she said.

"I have no time to entertain visitors."

She sat down.

He suddenly began to talk about the weather. "A very wet spring. The rivers will flood the fields. Is it so wet in Massachusetts?"

And in this way he went on for about ten minutes, now and then looking at her with a crafty glance to see if she was discomfited.

She interrupted him. "Mr. Butler, I did not come here to talk about the weather."

"Ah!"

She looked at him sternly. The crafty eyes stopped shifting for a moment.

"I want you to hear what I have come to say."

He leaned back with surprise to regard her, but she couldn't tell whether with scorn or with the faintest glint of admiration.

"I have come to bring before you certain facts involving terrible suffering to your fellow creatures all around you."

She rose as if delivering a judgment. "I want to bring before you certain facts, and my duty will end there. The rest"—she fixed him sternly with her glance—"shall be entirely your responsibility."

She showed him the articles in the *Providence Journal.* He pursed his lips. He had read them.

In a low voice and without stopping, holding her eyes fixed on his, her hands pressed together, living the terrible scene over again, she told him the story of poor Simmons.

When she finished she heard for a moment only the tick of the clock, and Mr. Butler's asthmatic breathing in the depths of the dusty chair.

He stirred, wet his lips, wiped the corners of his mouth with his finger tips. Then, lifting one withered lid, he gave her an odd glance.

"What do you want from me?"

She swallowed. "Thirty thousand dollars!"

No answer came from the depths of the chair. The clock went on ticking.

"How much did you say?"

"I said thirty thousand dollars, Mr. Butler."

He sat forward, pressed his finger tips together, sucked in his cheeks, and drew his mouth into a knot. "Quite a sum, Miss Dix."

He scratched his nose. "I like big enterprise, Miss Dix."

He stroked his chin, looked at the ceiling. "You shall have it."

He called the butler, and wrote a check. She folded it into her reticule as if it might be a dollar bill, but her knees trembled.

At the door she said, "We shall name the hospital after you. It will be called Butler Hospital."

He made a chuckling sound, almost like the coo of a baby. "Why didn't you tell me before?"

"We don't buy acts of conscience, Mr. Butler."

Outside, Mr. Hall waited for her.

She showed him the check.

He gazed at her, aghast. "How did you do it?" he asked. "How . . . ? By what means?"

She felt weak, almost faint. "Faith in mankind."

"Faith," said the minister, "how often I forget!"

Behind them a face, wrinkled like a walnut, peered

out of the window for a moment. Then the old, dusty lace curtain fell again.

The building of Bulter Hospital began that spring. But poor Simmons passed beyond mortal suffering long before the new building was completed.

Letters of supplication came to Dorothea from every state. She went on to New York, and then to New Jersey, hearing of one case of dire suffering and then of another.

7

"My First Child"

Two years later, on a winter day, Dorothea turned in from State Street in Trenton to the icy slope which led to the state capitol. At the foot of the slope lay the old stone barracks from which Washington had marched. Beyond looped the frozen Delaware.

She passed between the marble columns, pulled open a heavy door, went down a long hall, and in one of the offices behind the Senate chamber she found a gentleman waiting for her.

Wearily she put down a sheaf of papers on his table. "Senator Dodd," she said, "I have at last finished my *Memorial to the New Jersey Legislature.*

"I have investigated five hundred cases of human suffering. I have found the usual cases of horror—

a man in a shed no bigger than a coffin, several people frozen to death this winter for lack of care."

The senator, a stout, kindly man of fifty, shuddered. "Such facts should wring some small measure of sympathy from our hardhearted legislators."

"A small measure will not do!" Dorothea told him firmly.

His expression changed. "I have told you before, Miss Dix, it will take time and patience."

"Those who suffer cannot be asked to be patient."

"Miss Dix"—the senator rose to face her—"you do not understand the legislators of New Jersey. I have been a member of the medical committee for ten years.

"For ten years I have pleaded, for ten years our governors have pleaded that something be done for the plight of the suffering insane.

"Miss Dix"—he took a turn through the room; returned to her; faced her, spreading out his hands on his desk—"in those ten years, how do you think the legislature replied?

"In ten years' time they voted us five hundred dollars! For what? For a survey to show that the needs of the insane poor could be met quite adequately without intervention by the state!

"Imagine, Miss Dix! In ten years our state legislature has not voted one dollar, has not given one bed, has not furnished one garment for a mentally sick person in this state."

"Excellent! Excellent!" Dorothea cried.

"Miss Dix, this is no time for sarcasm."

"I speak most seriously, Senator Dodd. Your situation is ideal."

"Ideal, ma'am?" He gazed at her as if she had taken leave of her senses.

She leaned over the desk and began talking rapidly with great excitement. "Don't you see, Senator Dodd, that here in New Jersey you have an ideal situation?"

He shook his head.

"Of course! Of course!" she cried. "When I began to work in Massachusetts, a hospital already existed. We had only to enlarge it.

"When I went to work in Rhode Island, the ground had already been purchased and the plans existed for the institution we know now as the Butler Hospital.

"When they called me to work in New York, the Utica Hospital already existed. All I could win was an appropriation from the legislature to build some extra rooms.

"But here, Senator Dodd, as you have pointed out, you have no hospital. Not one dollar has been voted. Not one brick has been laid.

"Here, Senator Dodd," she cried with excitement,

"we can build a model hospital for the whole nation to see and copy."

He put his hands to his head. "I suppose you have already picked out the site?"

"Indeed!"

"And you have a plan in mind?"

"Of course."

"Without question you know the exact sum which the state legislature will vote us."

"A hundred and fifty thousand dollars."

"Impossible!" he cried.

She went to the window and stood silent for a moment. From the window she could see the old stone barracks, and the frozen bend of the Delaware.

She beckoned to the senator. Puzzled, he rose and stood beside her. She spoke quietly, as if seeing a scene enacted before her eyes.

"From those barracks George Washington marched with his ragged men on a day like this, to cross the frozen Delaware."

"Miss Dix, I can make speeches too!"

She turned to him, cold and hard. "Senator Dodd, on that day, as Washington passed with his barefoot men along State Street, people looking out of their windows must have said 'Impossible!'

"There's no such word!" she cried.

Two weeks later, on January 25, 1845, Senator

Joseph Dodd rose in the Senate to present a *Memorial* prepared by Miss Dorothea Lynde Dix, and a resolution asking for a hundred and fifty thousand dollars to build a model hospital in New Jersey.

Members of the Senate howled him down. One member, jumping on a chair, shouted, "Let's vote the sum of a thousand dollars—"

"Hear! Hear!" cried the other members. "What for?"

"To carry Miss Dix across the Delaware, and get her out of the state!"

"Hear! Hear! It would be worth a thousand dollars!"

This jibe repeatedly found its way into the newspapers. A cartoon showed Dorothea being carried on a rail across the Delaware.

Senator Dodd came to see Dorothea in her boardinghouse on State Street. "I know the legislature. I know those men!"

Dorothea said quietly to him, "They are human. They have minds that can reason, and hearts that can be reached."

"Ha!" He made a gesture of disgust.

"Bring them to me, one by one or in groups."

"They won't come."

She rose, smiling. "Not to be convinced, but to laugh at me, to gaze at me with curiosity. Oh yes, they'll come; just invite them."

He gazed at her amazed, shook his head, and went

out. For a whole month, evening after evening, she met hostile legislators in her landlady's front parlor.

They questioned her, criticized her, told her she knew nothing about politics; that she did not understand the people of New Jersey, nor their practical problems.

"After all, ma'am," one said in a patronizing voice, "you come from Massachusetts."

"After all," another one said, "it's the way of a woman to be softheaded." He had meant to say "softhearted." The others all laughed and, to their surprise, so did she.

On a very cold night, late in February, Mr. Dodd brought the last of the legislators, among them one of the most hostile.

"Tonight," he whispered as the others took off their wraps in the hall, "I have brought you the worst one of all, the man who shouted 'Humbug' when your bill came up. And I am afraid that he will shout 'Humbug' tonight!"

As the visitors, all members of the House, came into the parlor, Dorothea saw that one of them, a dark-haired fellow hunched like a buffalo, glowered at her from the back of the room.

"Gentlemen," she said in her soft, nonchallenging voice, "I have gathered certain facts which I would like to put before you.

"I shall make no efforts to convince you, gentlemen. I have no powers to convince. I have no power of oratory, gentlemen. I speak to you only as men kind enough to come out on a cold night to visit a woman who is a stranger in your midst, and who has been called by many, perhaps, an intruder.

"Forgive me, gentlemen–I do not mean to intrude. And I wish on this cold night that I could be sitting by my own fireside, knitting; looked after perhaps by a husband, surrounded by my own sweet children.

"Gentlemen, your wives are fortunate to have such a destiny. I am a woman alone. I have no husband. I have no children.

"Do you begrudge me, therefore, gentlemen, that I take to my heart suffering mankind; that I come with my poor powers here to New Jersey to plead their cause?

"Gentlemen, outside there is a cold wind blowing from the Delaware. Washington marched with his men on such a night, and his men left blood on the street which passes this house.

"Gentlemen, you came up State Street in your great-coats lined with fur. Some of you wore heavy capes and woolen shawls besides.

"Gentlemen, on such a night the insane poor in the Shark River poorhouse lie without heat, bedding, or covering in a shed penetrated by the wind.

"I know, gentlemen. Several froze to death this winter. And before this cruel wind dies down, perhaps tonight, others may freeze!"

Several men twisted in their seats. One man sat with his head sunk between his shoulders. The wind tore at the windows and swayed the stiff rubber plant in front of the lace curtains. The Franklin stove sputtered with a moan.

The burly man at the back of the room rose like a buffalo about to charge. "Madam, I do not wish to hear another word. Do you hear me? Not another word."

He pushed his way to the door, paused; turned around, his heavy dark face twisted with an emotion which was not exactly rage. It seemed as if he were about to cry.

"I am convinced. You have conquered me!"

He took out a mammoth handkerchief and blew a blast that rattled the shutters. "If you'll come to the House, and talk there as you've done here, no man that isn't a brute can stand you!"

He blew another tremendous blast. "I'll vote for your hospital bill."

He blew once more. "When a man's convinced, that's enough!"

He disappeared into the hall. The door slammed so that the house shook. Then the door opened again.

He poked his head into the parlor, blew his nose again.

"Lord bless you, Miss Dix!" he cried, and disappeared.

The hospital bill passed with a big majority in both houses. In April, Dorothea went with a committee to pick out the site for the New Jersey State Hospital.

She had already sought out a site a few miles from Trenton—a hundred rolling acres sweeping down with a beautiful vista toward the shining Delaware.

She stood on a hilltop looking down at this view. She dreamed of the building which had been growing on the architect's plan. Nowhere in the world had such a building been built for the mentally sick.

She could see the central structure of pink Tuscan sandstone, with a gracious portico of white marble columns, from which would rise a tranquil dome and white spire of hope.

She could see the wings stretching out on either side of this building like arms of welcome. She could see the sunny rooms, the wide beautiful halls, the lovely curving stairways. She could see sick men and women being treated with loving-kindness. Her eyes filled with tears as she thought of this place of hope.

"My first child," she murmured.

She went on to Pennsylvania. There, investigating

the plight of insane people held in prisons, she saw the plight of criminals.

Long there had lain in her mind the horror of those cells in East Cambridge which looked down, day and night, upon the gallows.

Long there had lain in her heart the anguish of those prisoners who had to look down on their fellows who died, swinging in air, upon the scaffold—a shadow which persisted when the rope swayed empty, for who can forget such sights?

She had not spoken then in East Cambridge. She had had no strength to speak, except to beg for a stove for the indigent insane held in the basement.

Now she dared to speak for the unloved, sullen criminals as Howard of England had done. "They are human too!" she cried. "No matter that they have offended."

For a summer she deflected from her work of helping the insane. Instead she visited jails and prisons all over the state of Pennsylvania.

She saw men beaten and lashed. She saw men held in solitary confinement until they lost their reason. She saw them filthy, brutalized.

She visited the Allegheny County Jail in Pittsburgh and found "transgressors of all ages, colors, men and women and little children, all promiscuously associated."

She found the "sick unattended, the ignorant untaught, the repentant unencouraged, and the mentally morbid forgotten. If it had been the deliberate purpose of the citizens of Allegheny County to establish a school for vice, they could not have better succeeded than under those conditions which I discovered in full operation in the jail last August."

She wrote these facts in an article for the *Pittsburgh Daily Gazette and Advertiser*, asking that men of heart look into the stench, horror, and moral evil of prisons "which do not correct, but transgress against human beings."

The Mayor of Pittsburgh, Mr. William J. Howard, appointed a committee which made recommendations to the legislature. The legislature took no action.

Dorothea wrote her thoughts into a manual which she called simply *Some Remarks on Prisons and Prison Discipline*. She called for the humane treatment of criminals. "They also suffer from a morbidity, which may perhaps yield to kind treatment."

She called for "well-lighted cells, food to nourish, chaplains and doctors to care with mercy for those who have sinned against society."

She asked for "steady, firm and kind government of prisoners," for "wardens who shall be more than keepers. We need molders of men."

She sent a copy of these writings to Horace Mann

and to Dr. Samuel Gridley Howe—both members of the Boston Prison Society, which had long agitated for reform.

The society published Dorothea's manual, of which Horace Mann said, "For her thoughts on prisons alone, Dorothea Lynde Dix is entitled to a place in history."

It seemed to her that centuries had passed since she had written the impetuous letter pouring out her heart to Horace Mann. Now she had no personal life.

She resumed her investigation of the plight of the insane in Pennsylvania. She presented a *Memorial to the Pennsylvania Legislature*. She fought, persuaded, and pleaded with legislators again.

She secured the money to build another model hospital. A building of rosy brick, with Tuscan portico and wings stretching out like arms of welcome, rose at Harrisburg.

"My second child!" she murmured.

8

Many Rivers

Beyond Pennsylvania lay the Alleghenies; beyond the Alleghenies, the opening West. The first rail lines had stretched around the mountains. The first canals had cut through.

A tremendous population poured westward—men seeking opportunity; women with children; the old and the young, the sick and the tormented, for whom no one had time to care.

In the new, raw towns roaring with the sound of saws and hammers, who had time to build hospitals? Who had time to think of those who could not succeed, or who fell by the way?

Dorothea went West, a pilgrim with a portmanteau, a Samaritan in petticoats, a voice to plead in the wilderness. She traveled over swollen rivers. Once her horse was almost swept downstream. She traveled through forests. Once her coach was held up by a highwayman. A man in a mask, with a pistol held in a hand like steel, he ordered all the passengers out.

Dorothea dared to ask him, "Do you know what you are doing?" But her voice was not angry, only sad.

The gun wavered. "I've heard that voice before!" he cried. "Once in a prison in Pennsylvania someone spoke like that, with kindness. I know who you are, Dorothea Lynde Dix."

He waved the gun. "Get back into the coach, and be on your way, all of you. I will not stop Miss Dix." He hesitated a second. "No one can stop Miss Dix."

Then he wheeled and rode into the forest.

Dorothea went from state to state in the opening West. She ranged the Mississippi River in a side-wheeler, and the Ohio. She traveled as far north as Canada, as far south as Louisiana.

She visited jails, almshouses, prisons. She prepared *Memorials* which she presented in state after state. Simultaneously she had five *Memorials* before five states–Kentucky, Indiana, Illinois, Tennessee, and Ohio.

Dorothea wrote to her friend Mrs. Rathbone in England, from a flatboat on the tributary of the Ohio, in the summer of 1846, "I have traveled more than ten thousand miles. I have visited eighteen state penitentiaries, three hundred county jails and houses of correction; more than five hundred almshouses, hospitals, and houses of refuge."

In September, 1846, while visiting a hospital in Columbus, Ohio, she collapsed. She lay ill in a boardinghouse for many months.

She wrote to Ann Heath, "My robe of life is travel-worn."

But letters of need came to her from all over the country. That December she wrote to Ann again, still from the bleak room of a boardinghouse in Columbus. "I have long thought of the great need to better the conditions of the insane sick who suffer greatly in many regions of the South."

She began her journeyings once more. She traveled by boat along the Ohio River to the Mississippi, then down the Mississippi from St. Louis to New Orleans. Then she took the upper passage along the Alabama River to Montgomery.

From Montgomery she traveled overland to Augusta; from Augusta to Georgia; from Savannah by coastal packet to Charleston, South Carolina; and then from South Carolina to North Carolina, "where I find," she wrote, "over a thousand persons, sick in their minds, who suffer in great want."

All along the way she had visited jails and prisons; all along the way she had presented *Memorials*. The legislature of Tennessee voted a hundred and fifty thousand dollars to "create a suitable hospital for the mentally sick of the state."

The Mississippi legislature passed a resolution on March 1, 1847, to "endow and build at Jacksonville a model hospital for the mentally tormented of our counties."

In Raleigh, North Carolina, where she took a room at the Mansion House near the capitol, Dorothea found herself looked upon as an intruder; a dangerous person; perhaps, being a Yankee, "an abolitionist."

She prepared a moving *Memorial* to be presented to the legislature, but could find not one legislator who would present it.

One man told her, "We need railroads, not hospitals."

Another man said, "If war should come over slavery, we shall need our money to fight the Union."

She finally called together, in the gold parlor of the hotel, a group of legislators whom she knew to be her enemies.

She read them her *Memorial*. She finished with the desperate final passage which has since gone down in history—the passage where, with a voice as of a prophet, she cried, "I am the hope of the poor crazed beings who pine in cells, and stalls, and cages, and wasterooms.

"I am the revelation of hundreds of wailing, suffering creatures hidden in your private dwellings, and in pens, and in cabins—cut off from all healing influences, from all mind-restoring solicitude; shut out from love.". . .

She read this passage and looked around. The men before her had not heard, had not felt. They puffed on cigars. They chewed on their pipes.

She pleaded. . . .

A man with a huge vest, an immense golden chain, and a manner of rather pompous gallantry rose. "Don't upset yourself, ma'am. We will introduce your bill."

She knew what he would do—introduce her bill and never bring it out of committee. Her bill would be killed with silence.

She gave the pompous gentleman her bill. What else could she do? She climbed the stairs to her room. She passed distracted down the hall carpeted in red and gold.

As she did so, she passed a half-open door from which came the sound of moaning. Without thinking she pushed open the door. A woman lay on the bed, delirious and tossing with fever.

Dorothea went to her at once. She wrung out a towel in cold water. She put the towel on the woman's forehead. She sat by the woman's bedside, changing the towels and smoothing the covers.

When she finally rose to go, the woman put out burning fingers. "Stay." Dorothea remained all afternoon nursing the sick woman. who evidently seemed to be in the last stages of consumption. She could not have been more than forty. Pathetically she clung to Dorothea.

Toward evening a man, quite evidently the woman's husband, stood in the doorway. "How is she?" he whispered anxiously.

Dorothea put her fingers to her lips. "Asleep."

She tiptoed out into the hall to talk to the tall, dark-eyed man with hollow temples and a harassed expression on his face. He seemed overcome with weariness.

"You are an angel of mercy," he said to Dorothea.

He told her that he came from Fayetteville, where he had not dared to leave his wife alone. "And the doctor told me it would make no difference if I brought her with me to Raleigh.

"Still I did not want to come. I did not want to move her. But it was her dying wish that I should come and do my duty."

"Who are you?" Dorothea asked.

"James Dobbin, a member of the legislature."

He turned to Dorothea. "And you?"

"Dorothea Lynde Dix."

For several weeks Dorothea nursed the sick woman,

forgetting her mission to the legislature; forgetting everything but the memory of her own illness long ago at Greenbanks, and the tenderness with which Mrs. Rathbone had nursed her then.

Dorothea sat up nights by the sickbed. She stayed by the woman whole days, sometimes not even taking the time to eat or to lie down for a moment.

One afternoon, toward twilight, the ragged, jagged breathing became smooth again, the sick face tranquil. Mrs. Dobbin turned to Dorothea, her head not burning with fever, her expression serene.

"I want to grant a wish for you, dear friend," she said, "a wish close to your heart."

Dorothea turned her face away.

"I asked my husband . . . I asked him . . ." But suddenly the fever began again, and the woman gasped for breath.

A few hours later she died, so suddenly her husband could not even be summoned. Dorothea traveled to Fayetteville with James Dobbin for the burial.

Afterward she urged him to stay and rest at his home—avoiding further sessions of the legislature, which would soon close for the Christmas holiday."

"I have work to do!" he said.

Of that work she was to hear later. On December 23, James Dobbin rose in the assembly, a black band of mourning on his arm, tears in his eyes.

"Gentlemen," he said, "I have just buried my wife. I bring you her dying wish. She wished—" he broke down. "She wished—"

He began again, trying desperately to calm himself. "Let me tell you of the angel of mercy who nursed her. Her name was Dorothea Lynde Dix.

"Gentlemen, I have come to ask you to vote for the hospital bill. I ask you not for myself, but in the name of my wife.

"It was her dying wish."

In the stillness of the house someone proposed, "I move the bill." Someone else called, "I second." The roll call began.

"Aye . . ."

"Aye . . ."

"Aye . . ."

So on December 23, 1848, in the State House at Raleigh, it was voted that North Carolina provide the sum of one hundred thousand dollars to build a model hospital for the mentally sick.

Dorothea went with the committee to pick the site, just outside of Raleigh—a slope of green land overlooking a beautiful valley and a river. Always she had loved the sight of flowing water.

"May we name the hospital after you, Miss Dix?" someone proposed.

"Not after me," she said, shielding her eyes from